Reborn

Adrianna Marie Ocampo

BookLeaf Publishing

India | USA | UK

Presentation by *BookLeaf Publishing*

Web: www.bookleafpub.com

E-mail: info@bookleafpub.com

ISBN: 9789357444705

First edition 2022

DEDICATION

To my son who I wish to inspire one day.

Stuck

Click, click, click.
Day after day. I click and flick and drink the waves of endless promotions. I eat my pictures before my food. I embody the woman on the cover of "what if". I struggle to one up the penniless man on my screen. The air is gray like my mind. The new green is blue light. My life is mass produced and still in production. Never to be released from the strings on my hands. The chains on my feet I drag from home to my job. My job is at home. I lick the cold brew dripping out of my cup. Card in hand ready for the next one. Life is not life without proof. Life was not my life now compared to mine before me. Life. Can. Be. Left. Behind.

brick roads blister feet

I don't know why I try. I don't know where I belong, I've been walking on this beaten road. Quiet and stable, I'm waiting for the tide to begin. Don't know how to answer the ad on these machine bred lives. I don't want to be here anymore, I want to live out of sight. I want to run where the trees can hide me. Feel my bare feet touch the earth and recharge my soul, the sun fills my energy's totem ready to live among the wild ones. I am a wild one.

Tame

Don't tame me, for I am fearless. Don't emulate
me, I am one of a kind. Take your fears and
expel them. For you are among a wild one.
There is no need to resign yourself to displaying
a fulfilled life.

As I say these words once again to myself, I start
to believe them.

Soil

As I walk the path between the earth and my skin, I gaze at this bucolic land, I splash the puddles with my feet on my way to the river. Pitter pat, crunch of grass I see mushrooms. Small and white speckled, eyes like drops of water gaze. Silently poking at me. They win. Up my foot, and we walk. Are things the way they seem? Obviously never, anywhere we go. Perspective shields the eyes, is it all bad? Can we choose, Which perspective we prefer to lose? Maybe this field of land they call fantasy is what they choose not to see. Unless…the land chooses not to lose me.

Bear yourself

Mushrooms on my shoulder. Feet blistered
almost to the river. I hear a million beads falling
into each other. We fly to the river, bleeding feet
but worth the work to get here.

Smells become distinct in seclusion. Wet, warm,
bloody, sharp, and furry. Feel the breath on the
top of your hair while the necks stand up.
Turning, counting, no. Holding on to breath like
I hold onto my life. As tall as the trees, I gaze.
Breath is now pleating, I want to scream.
Before the internal siren goes external. He sits.
He stares. He opens his paw and gruffs. First the
sight of blood then the shield goes over my eyes
once again to expose me to the offering.
Offering? Pink, meaty, raw, but thoughtful.
Food.

Still Starving I see Jumping pink, turquoise, and
green! Flying like a seagull so close to the water.
Warping my arms flopping about, impatient and
uncoordinated. Gruff again, wide mouthed catch
2. I am grateful. He offers again. Not to share
but to give in full. I bow in thanks. My guilt

starts to plead for forgiveness, as I have shielded my eyes from the blood and bones, choosing to see the protection of my new friend.

Calling for the unseen

Mushrooms jump out of hand, their caps rubbing together to make a chime. Ring the bell to

Dragonflies or dragons that fly these kept secret little winged creatures, zip through the sky so quick like when we blink the day away. This is nature's beauty between the cracks of her trees, river water, and moss on big boulder-like statues. They fly and up close illuminate like a rainbow in the sky. Their teeth small yet sharp, curved like rose thorns. The mushrooms burrow dry leaves and no longer in use branches. Our new friends spit and a brisk sharp poof of fire comes out. Like anything a single match compares nothing to a pit of fire. This place creates bits of home for me. Water to drink and wash. Friends to associate with. Fire to keep warm and cook this pink flesh.

Prices

Peace comes at a price. It is selective whether or not you want to see the new baby while an old life has passed. Tragedy comes in waves yet I am just getting. Started. Cold wind, freezing and wet as the sky cries on me. What tragedy have I overlooked during my introduction into this wonderland? Gruffs and growls lead me to a cave. The earth is warm, nature has warmed this soil for us to find peace at night. Peace comes at a price. But can tragedy be spun into beauty?

Morning

The tears have prevailed and my friends wake me to leave the dark and experience the bountiful mask of light. Nature's warm arms have greeted me this shines day. I can feel the wind but I ignore it because I am too excited. Run to the river. No fish this early, my senses smell, see then touch the flowers next to me. I have overlooked one thing. My (enter new term for mushrooms) friends have led me to an almond tree. What fun to see a berry bush next. I have overlooked what our mother gives. But today the light has shown through my ignorance and I can see more clearly. As morning continues to break through the trees and shower the air with sparkles in the air. We feast.

Hopes of a cloud

Soft yet fleecy
Untearable and also diminishing with a single
touch
bringing you closer to heaven feeling posh on
top of it
Knowing you can fall but when we fall there is
tranquility in the force of air
How immaculate the sun falls with me.
And i am in harmony, i am in high because if i
can not take it with me i will fall with the intent
of being in less pain then gravity pulling me to
my grave.

Deity

Higher power, Mother Nature, candle maker;
god above all else.. peace maker, making me
rebuild, rethink, relive. Past life's reborn, last
life's ends in scorn. I whip my integrity into the
water to drown. I let go of the bolder, and
breathe

Forbidden acts

Dancing in the rain,
Shouting in a small space,
Eating with manus,
Be silent and still,
Be unbound,
Let your hair down, and roll in the dirt.
Just be uncaged.

We all live on earth, who lives on Mars

As I sit, when I hear the silence I wait to see if there is someone in replacement, sitting in the same silence, some remorse, some anger with the world they think is everywhere except their living room, the room in which is not really where we live. Am I the only escaped prisoner? I'm sure I only think I am the only one, just me only me, yet I am not the only one running away. If only we were bound together in this universe to live on Mars together.

Backtrack decisions

I wonder if I can go back. Will I feel the same? Am I homesick? Was I too quick to run? Do second chances run intwine with our first choices? Is it allowed? Am I still asleep waiting to wake up and feel an impossible feeling? Signs are waiting for recognition..

Blight

Spinning trees, body twisting, berry bad ideas. Slow winks, water burning inside, cherry on my skin. Lay to rest on the smooth rock. Resting my eyes. Just a moment. I wake with slow shallow breaths. Friends crawling up my arms, the soil is cold, with nauseating air. I turn in my fresh grave ready to let my roots settle for the last time. Close your eyes sweet child. Let the berry be white.

Elixirs

Water for rebirth,
Wood to rebuild,
Grass to help you grow,
Flowers to treasure beauty; laid on our casket,
Blood to give back,
Bodies equivalent to earth,
Organic, rare, sensitive, & dying.
I am the soil.

Last breath

No one will notice the wind until it has something to say, wind pipes loud and screaming to shelter yourself. Night winds warn of chilly nights. Stories to help you sleep deep until sunrise saves us with warm arms. Unless you think you're screaming and it's a cold winded breath, peeling the floor with your hands, nails filled with cold soil. Eyes closing, breath pleating, heart slowing by every breath.

I didn't know I would die like this.

Heaven is a warm place

Waking in a hay filled bolster,
wood sanded floor. Fire in the wall,
Body eliminating white murky water into a
bucket on the floor.
I gather myself.
"Eat, drink, rest." Shadow in the corner stool
sitting.
Jam. Bread. Liquor, on the table.
Reaching slowly, no more traps.
"Eat, eat!" He emerges.
White berries is a slow suicide, I feel warm,
greatful. In time we talk, an alien has emerged
on my earth, but little did I know he has lived
on mars for a decade and has doubts that with
my bad decision I can never leave my earth.
Mars is not an option, my homesickness is my
sign. Can I be forced back into a cage that was
unlocked with others who were too voided in
their own lives to see it was unlocked to begin
with?

Home again

I never noticed I was so close to Mars. I come home and there is an abundance Of robots that I no longer know. I did not know this could look more dull than I had imagined before. But the sky is darker, grass is faker. Things taste pale and lifeless. Can it be that I have made my decision before this journey began? I miss my new friends. I have a lost soul, I do not belong on Mars, I belong with me.

Self worth

My self worth is so much more than what I realized. I run to the water, trees, dirt, caves, forest. I chirp for my friends. To congregate along with each other. I'll make the fire and taste the berries again and if I poison myself I will know I am giving myself to me, my earth, my Mars. I am worth so much more to myself than to society's mask of bound people chanting and changing nothing. I am not free, I am just fitting in the life I choose for me. I am happy.

www.ingramcontent.com/pod-product-compliance
Lightning Source LLC
LaVergne TN
LVHW050307200726
843509LV00015B/3205